THE LEGEND

OF THE

EMPTY BOWL

FRANCES JONES

ILLUSTRATED BY CHRISTOPHER WANER

insight
PUBLISHING GROUP

Tulsa, Oklahoma

THE LEGEND OF THE EMPTY BOWL

The Legend of the Empty Bowl by Frances Jones
Published by Insight Publishing Group
8801 S. Yale, Suite 410
Tulsa, OK 74137
918-493-1718

ISBN: 1-930027-92-3

Library of Congress catalog card number: 2003103047

Printed in the United States of America

DEDICATION PAGE

Dedicated to the children
who never have enough to eat
and those who care enough to help.

Special thanks to Barbara Knapp
who cares deeply about hungry children.

Ten-year-old Tommy didn't feel so well. It was the evening before Thanksgiving, and his head was hurting. His heart was aching as well.

Earlier that day, Tommy and his classmates had collected money to help feed hungry children during the holidays. As they sat and learned how and where their donations would be used, they also learned some startling facts.

"Poverty is quite a serious problem," Tommy's teacher said. "Worldwide, more than 153 million boys and girls go to bed hungry every night. (See statistic A on page 32.) Did you know that 13 million of those boys and girls live in the United States?" (See statistic B on page 32.) she asked. "That's one child out of every 5.5 (six). (See statistic C on page 32.) None of those kids will be eating Thanksgiving dinner tomorrow, much less eating breakfast Friday morning."

How can that be? Tommy wondered. *All the kids in my class have more than enough to eat at every meal no matter if it was Thanksgiving or just breakfast,* he thought.

Tommy listened and studied the posters hanging on his classroom wall. One poster showed a group of children in Africa sitting under a tree on the cracked, barren ground, holding up empty bowls, waiting for something to eat.

Another poster showed a group of shabbily dressed children living on a cold, damp street in eastern Europe, holding up empty bowls, waiting for something to eat. A third poster showed a group of children standing in front of a dusty shack in rural America, holding up empty bowls, waiting for something to eat. Tommy didn't fully understand why poverty existed, but he did know that he must help find an answer.

When Tommy arrived home from school later that day, not only was something gnawing at his stomach, something else was gnawing inside him. "I don't feel so good," he told his mom. "And I don't want any dinner. I'm just not hungry." Tommy's mother felt his forehead and decided that he didn't have a fever, so she let him lie on the couch to watch television.

It wasn't long, though, before Tommy felt even worse. The evening news ran a story about poverty and reported those same disturbing statistics Tommy had learned at school. He definitely wasn't hungry now. "I'm goin' to bed," he told his mom and dad. "This has been a terrible day." "Sleep well," they said, a little puzzled. "Tomorrow will be better. We're going to have lots of fun and lots of food, and all our family will be together for the first time in many, many years."

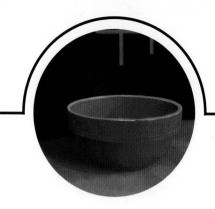

But Tommy didn't sleep well. He woke up, then snoozed, woke up, then snoozed, again and again. Finally, just before sunrise, Tommy slipped into a restless sleep. When Tommy's mom and dad woke up, they checked to see that he was still sleeping and shut his bedroom door to keep out the noise from the rest of the house.

Tommy's mom busied herself in the kitchen making pumpkin pie and putting the turkey and stuffing into the oven. Tommy's dad built a fire in the fireplace and watched the holiday parades on TV. Soon, it started to get warm in the house. But with his bedroom door closed, it was still chilly in Tommy's room.

Fast asleep, he began to dream he was one of the hungry children he had seen on a poster; a child without a home or a family, living alone on the streets. As his blanket slipped off his shoulders, he dreamt he had no heavy clothes to keep him warm. Tommy shivered as he walked against a frigid wind. He could feel the hard, cold sidewalk through the holes in his shoes. If only he had a coat or a jacket instead of a thin, tattered shirt; why, even a sheet of cardboard to wrap around his shoulders would keep the cold away.

Tommy dreamed that some bigger kids bullied him and stole the few pennies he had in his pockets. And although he was scared, he sensed something far worse than fear—he felt hunger. He couldn't remember the last time he had eaten a nourishing meal.

But wait? What was that smell? In his dream, Tommy remembered that same aroma from years ago—before he needed safe shelter, before his father died and his mother got sick and couldn't work. That was when Tommy always had a warm meal to eat. He followed the delicious scent. What exactly was it? Turkey, gravy, pumpkin pie?

Still fast asleep, Tommy dreamed that he had come to a small building. Gold lettering spelled Angel's Café across a big front window. He peeked through the panes. A lady was preparing food for Thanksgiving.

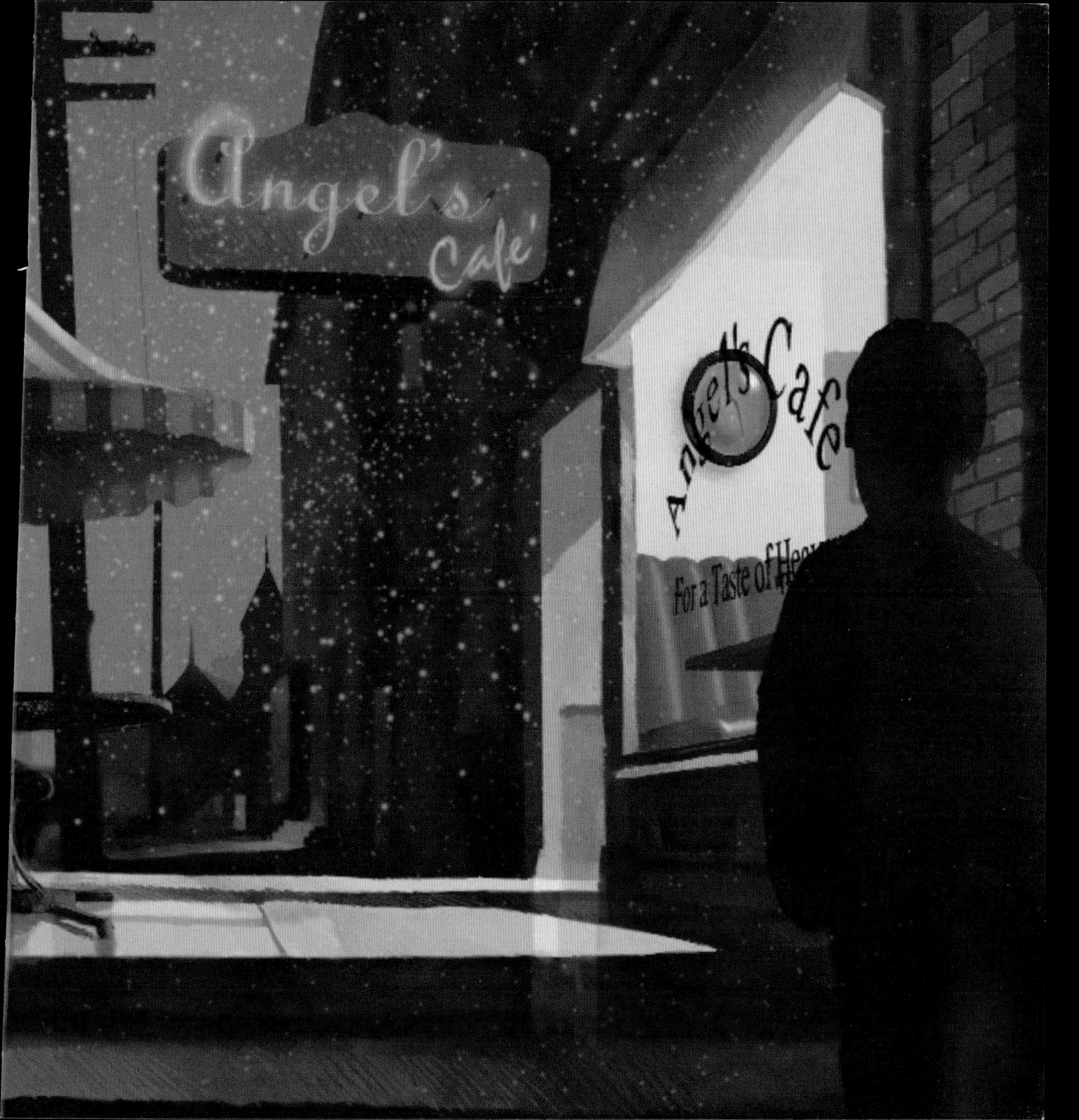
Angel's Café
Angel's Cafe
For a Taste of

When she looked outside, she saw Tommy pressed against the window. "Are you hungry?" she asked as she opened the door to the café. The lady invited Tommy to a counter where she warmed him up, cleaned him up and cheered him up. She then handed Tommy a bowl of food, which he gobbled down.

He held up his empty bowl and asked for more and more and more, and the lady gave and gave and gave until Tommy was full. "Are you an angel?" he asked. "The sign says 'Angel's Café.'" "No," the lady replied as she took off her new sweater and pulled it down over Tommy's frail shoulders, "that's just a nick-name Grandma gave me when I was small. But I like to think that God uses me, as He might use an angel." "Whadda you mean?" "Tommy, do you know the verse in the Bible where Jesus says to 'Love God and love your neighbors as well?'"

Tommy shook his head no. "Well," the lady replied as she took off her new shoes and slipped them on Tommy's chilly feet, "it's a verse that has become my way of life. I love God, and I show Him how much I love Him by loving my neighbors." "You mean the people living next door?" "No," the lady answered, giving Tommy a big smile and hug. "Neighbors are anybody, anywhere in the world, who need help—like you. We're all part of God's family."

Suddenly, the doorbell rang, and Tommy woke up. He looked around his bedroom and realized he had been dreaming. He heard his aunts and uncles laughing in the living room. And that wonderful smell of food in the air? It was coming from his own kitchen! Tommy dressed quickly and joined his family for Thanksgiving dinner.

As they gathered around the table to thank God for their blessings, Tommy asked if he could tell everyone about his dream. "I learned somethin' really important last night," Tommy said. He hurried into the kitchen, got a bowl from the cabinet and set it on the table. "This bowl is empty right now, just like the bowls of millions of boys and girls around the world."

"This bowl will stay empty unless an angel fills it. I may be just a kid, and I may not be able to do much. But I'll do what I can. I'm gonna do extra chores around the house and put part of my weekly allowance into this bowl. Then, every year at Thanksgiving, I'm gonna take that money and make sure hungry boys and girls have food to eat. We're all family here, but our neighbors in the world are part of God's family too, and they need our help."

Tommy kept his word, and thus an annual tradition began. Thirty years later, on Thanksgiving day, five empty bowls sit on Tom's table—one for himself, one for his wife, one for his daughter, and one for each of his two sons.

The bowls represent the children Tom and his family will help feed during the coming year. Tom had found an answer to the problem of poverty that had troubled him in elementary school. He and his family would always care and share because there would always be "neighbors" who need help and hope.

Many, many children, maybe hundreds, even thousands in the United States and overseas have had their empty bowls filled because of the love of God a ten-year-old boy received so long ago, the night a lady filled his bowl at Angel's Café.

STATISTICS

A. "More than 840 million people in the world are malnourished — 799 million of them are from the developing world. <u>More than 153 million of them are under the age of 5</u>. *Source: State of Food Insecurity in the World 2002. Food and Agriculture Organization of the United Nations.*

B. "Even in the most prosperous times, 33 million people, including <u>13 million children, in the United States</u> did not have access to enough food for an active healthy life, and were often forced to choose between relying on the emergency food sources or going hungry." *Source: Household Food Security in the United States, 2001. ERS Food Assistance and Nutrition Research Report No. FANRR-29, United States Department of Agriculture, October 2002.*

C. Population of children under 18 in U.S.= 70,925,261. *Source: U.S. Census Data, formatted for online use by KIDS Count, a program of the Annie E. Casey Foundation Web site; <u>http://www.aecf.org</u>. Jan. 2003.*

YOU CAN MAKE A DIFFERENCE

You can help meet the needs of children worldwide. Feed The Children has offices in 14 countries overseas, where we provide food. Children come to feeding centers because they have nowhere else to turn.

Please take a moment to consider how you can make a difference in the life of a child.

Feed The Children
P.O. Box 36
Oklahoma City, OK 73101
Phone: 1-800-627-4556, Ext. 4180
Web site: <u>www.feedthechildren.org</u>